My Best Friend

My Best Friend

Hallmark Editions

My Best Friend

My Best Friend must be

the _Best_ Best Friend

in the whole wide world,

and the kindest, and the funniest,

and the most understanding.

My Best Friend

is the kind of companion

I'm always happy to be with.

She's like a new person every day,

full of fresh ideas

and enthusiasm for living.

She can make a party come to life

just by walking in the door.

She can take some

of the sting out of sad times

just by being there,

just by caring.

My Best Friend always knows
what I'm talking about—
sometimes before I say it.

She seems to understand

all my moods so well.

If I'm feeling kind of blue,

she always has a sympathetic ear.

She says, "Tell me about it…"

and that always helps.

And if I'm feeling like acting silly,

she never tells me to get serious.

We act silly together!

I love our little private jokes.

All she has to say is

"Remember that time when..."

and we both break into laughter.

And it's really amazing how often

we like the same things

and the same people.

So often, it seems, we react alike

to the same situations.

If something worrisome comes along,

she assures me,

"It's going to be all right..."

and you know, it usually is!

She restores my perspective, too,

whenever I get too serious

about anything.

If my Best Friend had a garden full of roses

she would cut her loveliest blooms for me,

that's just the way she is —

generous, giving, loving.

We can be honest with each other,

there is no sham, no pretense.

If she pays me a compliment,

I know she means it.

If she says, "How's everything with you?"

she really <u>wants to know</u>—

she is concerned,

she is interested.

Sometimes I have a special project

confronting me

that seems more than I can manage,

but she says,

"No problem, let me help,

we'll do it together…"

and right away, it no longer seems

such a task.

I like to help her, too.

She is so appreciative.

That always makes it fun to do things

for your Best Friend,

and it gives you such a happy, good feeling.

My Best Friend and I

share so many things —

tangible and some intangible ones —

such as the wonders of Nature —

sunsets, the beauty of a garden,

a tree in autumn.

People who don't have

one Best Friend

really miss a lot.

I can't imagine getting along

without mine.

It seems as if we have

always been together,

sharing secrets and special plans…

calling each other

just to say "hello"

and going on shopping sprees.

We sometimes share our childhood memories

telling each other fun things

and sad things

that happened to us when we were little.

Sometimes we spend quiet moments together,

when there is no need to talk.

We share silences,

understanding each other

without saying so.

That is, after all,

what friendship is all about—

being sensitive to each other's needs...

knowing there is someone

who is willing to share

the laughter

and the tears.

I could go on and on,

singing the praises

of My Best Friend.

I could mention all

the nice things she has done

for me through the years.

I could talk about her kindness

to others and how proud

I always am to be with her.

But there isn't room here

for all the good things

I feel about My Best Friend.

So I'll just end this

by saying how very glad

I am to have a Best Friend...